The 9½ Secrets of a
Great IT Organization

The *9¹⁄₂* Secrets *of a* Great IT Organization

Don't Do IT Yourself

Paul M. Ingevaldson

Published by Gary Slavin, Longwood, Florida

Printed in the United States of America

ISBN: 978-0-615-65155-2

Library of Congress Control Number: 2012941052

Managing Editor: Arthur H. Slavin

Edited by Brenda Judy
www.publishersplanet.com

Cover and Interior Design by Carolyn Sheltraw
www.csheltraw.com

Disclaimer: The example and company name used in Appendix B are fictitious. Any resemblance to an actual company or historical event is purely coincidental. Although the case study in Appendix C is factual, the fictitious name, Paul's Hardware, has been used to protect the privacy of the actual business.

♾ This paper meets the requirements of ANSI/NISO Z39.48-1992 (Permanence of Paper).

www.garyslavin.com

www.paulingevaldson.com

This book is dedicated to those
IT practitioners and IT users
who labor behind the scenes to
keep our systems running.

TABLE OF CONTENTS

Foreword ix

Acknowledgements xiii

Chapter 1 – From Punched Cards to Wireless 1

Chapter 2 – IT Reporting Structure. 7

Chapter 3 – The IT Steering Committee. 13

Chapter 4 – Long-Range Planning 23

Chapter 5 – A Defined System Development Process . . 27

Chapter 6 – Up-to-Date Hardware and Software 37

Chapter 7 – Commitment to Training 43

Chapter 8 – Dual Career Paths. 49

Chapter 9 – Disaster Recovery Planning 55

Chapter 10 – Status and Metrics Reporting 61

Chapter 11 – The Digitally Aligned Corporation 67

Appendix A – The 9 1/2 Secrets Scorecard. 73

Appendix B – Company XYZ IT Steering Committee . . .79

Appendix C – Catalog Automation Case Study. 83

Supplemental Reading. 89

About the Author 93

FOREWORD

Paul and I first met in 1970, working as computer programmers for one of the largest retailers in the United States. We both left this company at about the same time and tried to stay in touch as our careers progressed, but lost track of each other. Paul successfully climbed the ladder of Information Technology (IT) management, while I became involved in creating and delivering training for IT professionals, and eventually started my own training and business consulting company.

Well, thanks to today's social media, Paul and I were able to reconnect several years ago. While visiting my Web site, Paul noticed we were now doing similar work and were in agreement as to the importance of corporate alignment. So, when Paul contacted me to discuss his 9 1/2 secrets of a great IT organization and the importance of corporate goal alignment, I was more than mildly interested.

The subject of alignment to a corporation's objectives has been around for a long time. One of Paul's *Computerworld* articles published in 2004 stated that there is absolutely no reason to have misalignment if the IT department is properly set up and managed. In this article he concluded that misalignment still exists because most IT shops are not being managed properly. This fact was the driving force behind Paul's developing and documenting the 9 1/2 secrets.

The purpose of this book is to detail the steps required to build a successful IT organization. Some of them will ensure alignment, some will ensure a competent workforce, and some will suggest important internal procedures to create a well-run organization. At the heart of all of the secrets is the requirement for IT to involve the users. IT cannot be successful without the users, and both parties must figure out the best way to work together for the benefit of the entire organization. No department in the modern corporation can operate as a private fiefdom doing only what it wants to do.

Misalignment often arises when IT alone decides the automation agenda. In most successful companies, the officers and board approve the advertising plan, the marketing plan, the operating budget, and the sales plan. Why not the automation plan as well? It just doesn't make sense not to do this. Without guidance, it's possible that IT won't be addressing key corporate objectives.

If IT does not address the most important automation needs of the company, there is a strong possibility that the company will fall behind its competitors and lose competitive advantage. It is very important that IT participates in the determination of the IT agenda, but it is equally important that IT not be the final decision maker. The users, officers, and board should approve the automation agenda. If this is done correctly, IT should be properly aligned with the corporation. The objective of this book is to assist the reader, whether a user or IT professional, in understanding and accomplishing this alignment.

I would suggest that all IT professionals read this book to assess the nature of their organizations or to evaluate an IT department that they may be looking to join. I also recommend this book for corporate executives who are IT users, in an effort to better understand their IT department, gain a better understanding of the IT professional, and learn how to work together, not only to obtain goal alignment, but to gain the competitive advantage that a successfully run IT department can offer a company.

Users can apply the 9 1/2 secrets to evaluate their IT departments. In so doing, they will be able to participate in an interesting and constructive dialogue aimed at continuing best practices and modifying those less than perfect to assist in creating a great IT department. A third audience for this book is the board membership who is increasingly concerned about the production of their IT department. As security, privacy, and governmental regulations expand, the board should get involved in certain aspects of IT in order to ensure that proper procedures are being followed.

In essence, this is a book for everyone interested in developing, maintaining, and improving cohesiveness within an organization. IT can spell SUCCESS.

Gary Slavin
Trainer, Consultant, and Author of
Plan Your Success: Turn Your Dreams Into Reality
www.garyslavin.com

ACKNOWLEDGEMENTS

This book could not have been written without the wise counsel of Gary Slavin. He was a great sounding board for ideas and a great contributor to many of the concepts presented within the pages that follow. Gary and I have worked together in presenting the 9 1/2 Secrets in live seminars and in my classroom work, and he has been there along the way to help talk through concepts and provide his straightforward approach to presenting ideas.

Gary has also been instrumental in bringing this book to market by coordinating all aspects of the publishing process to include obtaining the editors and the design professionals. The expert editorial skills of Arthur Slavin and Brenda Judy, along with Carolyn Sheltraw's design skills, have definitely made this book better. I really thank Gary for all his hard work. I couldn't have done it without Gary and the editorial and design team.

Gary is a trainer, a consultant, and an author who operates his own training company in Florida, and I recommend his book, *Plan Your Success: Turn Your Dreams Into Reality.* By using his book, you can make an attempt to plan for that most unplanned event in your life—your success. Many people have followed his sage advice and found their success a little more attainable and achievable.

CHAPTER 1

From Punched
Cards to Wireless

I started my career in computing in 1965, working at a data processing service bureau in the afternoon, after my classes at the university. One of the jobs I was trained for was something called card cleaning. I would receive a deck of "IBM Cards" from the keypunch department and, by using a machine called a sorter, I would edit the cards to be sure that punches were present in the columns that were required and not present in those columns that had to be blank.

If I discovered a punch where one shouldn't have been, I would actually take a small red sticker and cover the hole. If a column needed a hole, I would go to the 001 manual keypunch and create the punch. How primitive that must sound to readers who have grown up in the age of wireless devices and full motion videos on computers.

I ended my career reporting to the CEO and having responsibility for the Information Technology (IT) department at Ace Hardware, along with the P&L responsibility for Ace's International business. In IT, we worked on Ace's Web site, Enterprise Resource Planning (ERP) systems, wireless networks, security intrusion detection, wireless picking systems, and other very interesting new technologies.

Although punched cards sound primitive by today's standards (many of my students have never seen one), they were state of the art in 1965. What is considered state of the art today will be looked at like punched card editing thirty years from now. The pace of technology innovation will continue to grow and grow at a rapidly increasing rate. Just trying to keep current with technology is a monumental task. This phenomenon was forecasted by *Future Shock* author Alvin Toffler, who famously said, "The illiterate of the 21st century will not be those who cannot read and write but those who cannot learn, unlearn and relearn." Some people just want a phone that is only a phone. Some don't want to adjust the blinking 12:00 on the DVD player. Others are sticking with books and avoiding using Kindle and Nook.

The same is true in the modern corporation. New technologies are being announced daily, and how to effectively use them is the content of endless articles:

- Should we use social networks to communicate with our employees? Our vendors? Our stockholders?

- Should we allow employees to bring their own technology into the company?

- Are ERP systems the answer to our technology needs, or should we use the cloud?

- Is the security we have on our systems sufficient, or are we exposed to a major system outage should our firewalls be penetrated?

- What systems do we need to develop in order to gain competitive advantage?

- Should we outsource and/or offshore?

- What is the future of telecommuting? Can we use it to reduce travel costs?

- What will be the impact of computer hardware on our future capital expenditure budgets?

- What will be the impact of nanotechnology and robotics on our manufacturing costs?

The list is never-ending and will continue to grow.

However, despite the rapidly changing nature of these technologies, there are basic underlying truths that must be incorporated into the governance of the IT department in order to ensure that the company is able to exploit these new technologies as effectively as possible. Where did the list come from? I first developed the list back in 1985 when I was immersed in running an IT organization. I even wrote an article outlining these ideas but never sought to publish it. Since then a lot has changed in the IT environment but, amazingly, the underlying principles that lead to a great IT department haven't changed. These universal truths form the basis of this book.

It is no different than in sports. Most of the grassroot secrets that lead to a championship are the same today as they were forty years ago. In baseball, the bats and the uniforms have changed but executing the basics are still of paramount importance. Can you get the bunt down? Can you hit the ball to the right side to move the runner to third? Can you get a hit with runners in scoring position? In football it's: Can you score inside the twenty-yard line? Can you convert on third down? Can you execute the two-minute drill?

Unfortunately, the basic rules to properly set up and run an IT department are cloaked in mystery. Imagine you were a senior staffer in an IT department and one day the CEO came to you and said that the CIO had been fired and you were being promoted to the CIO position. What would you do? Where would you go to find out how to do the job? I would guess that you would just take over the job and try to figure it out. One thing that you would probably not want to do is to run the department the same way as your predecessor did. I think this is what happens in most IT shops. The CEO and the CIO just make it up as they go along. Some things will work, some will not, and some things will change. Hopefully the company doesn't suffer through this learning process.

As you trudge down the difficult road of IT, you'll probably ask yourself one or more of these questions:

- How should IT interact with the rest of the company?

- Who should IT report to?

- How are projects selected?

- How do you attract and retain talented people?

- How do you protect yourself against outside attacks and acts of God?

- What is the process for developing systems?

- How much involvement should the users have in this process?

- How do we create a positive environment for IT in the company?

- Are there personnel practices that must be used to manage IT people that are not needed with other employees?

These are the most important questions that need to be answered in order to create and maintain a great IT department. The answers will be revealed during the discussion of the 9 1/2 secrets.

CHAPTER 2

IT Reporting Structure

The most important IT issue facing the CEO in the modern corporation is to decide the best way to structure the IT organization. Unfortunately, this decision is not an easy one primarily because the typical CEO has little experience in the inner workings of an IT department. Usually the CEO comes from finance, sales, or manufacturing. Seldom does the pedigree include a stop in IT. In addition, there are few IT professionals among his/her social circle.

So what is a CEO to do? Usually, there is a historical bias against IT based on previous experience. At some time in one's career, there was an IT project that went awry either by being significantly over budget, by being unsuccessful upon implementation, or both. It is probably fair to say that the IT department carried the majority of the blame for these results. Whether this blame was properly placed is a subject for a future discussion. Suffice it to say that the experience has probably somewhat poisoned the CEO's view of IT.

Therefore, the CEO usually finds it useful to have the IT responsibility report to some other officer on the top management staff. Historically, this has most frequently fallen on the shoulders of the Chief Financial Officer (CFO). There are several reasons for this. The CFO is comfortable with numbers and IT is oftentimes considered a numbers oriented department. In addition, financial systems are usually installed in all organizations making the CFO comfortable with their presence. Finally, the typical CFO welcomes IT since there seems to be a lot of common elements, such as involvement across all departments and the need for corporate viewpoints over the entire automation portfolio.

I would argue the exact opposite. I think that the CFO is probably the least appropriate executive to delegate responsibility for IT. First of all, the CFO should be a very risk adverse executive. No pinkie rings or weekends in Vegas for this person. Unfortunately, IT, just like advertising and marketing, is very risky. Will the ad campaign work; will the new product sell; will we make budget; will the new system using brand new technologies satisfy the user; will the new technology work? Many new, extremely successful systems on which I worked would have probably been quashed if I had reported to the CFO.

Sometimes the CEO delegates the IT responsibility to another C-level executive. This is also very dangerous. What tends to happen in these cases is that the systems that support this C-level executive tend to be the ones that are developed. I once worked at a company that had IT reporting to the operations department. Coincidentally, we had excellent operating systems. If IT reports to the CFO, financial systems are the number one priority. Although I've never heard of this, if IT would report to marketing, we would probably see tremendous marketing systems developed. This phenomenon is only natural in a boss-subordinate environment.

Most companies usually have the CFO and the legal department reporting directly to the CEO; I would argue that the same rationale should be used to have the Chief Information Officer (CIO) directly reporting to the top. This is Secret #1. The reasons are simple. First of all, the automation agenda must be deployed in a way that maximizes its value to the corporation. This would be the same reasoning that puts the finance department into this type of relationship. No one has the overall company view equivalent to the CEO. I will make a single exception. If the CEO is primarily looking outside the company and the Chief Operating Officer (COO) is managing the internal business, then the COO-CIO reporting relationship works well.

This reporting relationship also enables the CEO/COO to become more familiar with the vast possibilities of the IT resource. It is one thing to get reports, but it is a wholly different experience to see technology firsthand and begin to think about the vast possibilities that technology advancements may create. Shouldn't this area be the proper arena for top management to evaluate?

There is also a very selfish reason for this recommended reporting structure. Reporting to the CEO/COO makes the job easier. IT must often engage in disruptive change. Oftentimes this change will affect many people in the organization including certain C-level executives. If IT is on the same level as these affected bosses, there is a much better chance of success. If IT is in a subordinate position, the internal politics will usually put roadblocks in front of truly innovative and business changing applications.

This high-level reporting structure will have another very important result. It will put IT on the map. It is sad to say that IT does not have a very good reputation within a lot of corporations. Many people consider it a utility that does the bidding of the corporation. In these situations, it is hard for IT to garner the respect that it needs to be the agent of change that is necessary. Reporting to the CEO/COO will also enable the company to find highly qualified CIOs that can take the ball and run with it. These types of candidates will not be attracted to companies that have a low opinion of IT.

This is a self-fulfilling prophecy in most corporations. Have a low opinion of IT and have it reporting low in the corporation and you will get an IT utility that is not innovative or assertive of its abilities. Have IT report high in the organization and you will attract top talent that will take IT and the company to new heights and market share. You will get what you pay for.

There is another necessary requirement enabling this type of reporting relationship to be successful. The CIO must be the type of executive that knows how to report to the highest levels of the corporation. The CIO must understand how the company operates and know what major success factors the company must achieve. He/she must know how the company makes money, how it approaches its market, and the nature of its competition. In other words, the CIO must have the same business acumen that would be expected of any other C-level executive. If the only things that come out of the CIO's mouth are technical jargon that is unintelligible, then the position will never attain its proper place in the organization.

Looked at in a different way, the CEO/COO should only place a CIO in this position if he/she is capable of working at this level. Most CEOs have learned that you don't necessarily put the best accountant in the CFO's job or the best marketing manager into the Chief Marketing Officer's (CMO) job. However, some CIOs are rewarded with the CIO's job primarily due to their technical expertise. This is unacceptable and leads to many of the horror stories we hear about inept IT management.

The CIO position should be looked upon in the same way as any other C-level position. If there is no one internally that can fill the bill, don't pick the "best of the rest." Either look outside for a qualified candidate or look internally in other departments for someone who is intelligent, a fast learner with curiosity, and someone who understands the business.

Once again, the advice is to look at IT and the CIO as just another part of the business that happens to use technology to accomplish its goals. The CIO should be a businessperson first and a technologist second. If that is done, then IT has a much better chance of integrating effectively into the business.

CHAPTER 3

The IT Steering Committee

The usual reaction of companies without a Steering Committee is, "Why does IT need one? We don't do this for other departments. Doesn't IT know what to do?" There is an easy answer for this and there is also a more complicated one. We will discuss both in this chapter.

The easy answer is this. We need an IT Steering Committee because "completed IT systems do NOT belong to IT, they belong to the user." This is a fundamental difference between the output of the IT department and the output of any other department. In other departments, they own the product of their labors. In IT, the user owns the completed system. IT develops the system and then turns it over to the user.

As for the complicated answer, one of the biggest problems facing IT management is the subject of alignment. In the latest survey of CIOs conducted by *CIO* magazine, alignment was identified as their most critical problem. This problem occurs when IT develops systems that are not the systems the company feels it needs to conduct its business. It's as if IT decides on its own what it should automate and on what schedule. This is absurd. This problem arises when company management believes IT should be smart enough to understand the needs of all of the departments of the company and also understand the time frames in which the systems are needed.

Of course, this is ridiculous. No CIO worth his/her salt should allow this to happen. And no CIO is that brilliant (although I'm sure that there are some who think they are). The automation needs of the company must be tied to the strategic plan, and the execution of the strategic plan is the job of the corporate officers of the company. So, the decision becomes a simple one. Let IT determine the automation agenda and risk having a misaligned automation plan, or have the IT Steering Committee approve an automation plan that is the result of a consensus of all the corporate officers. If the latter is selected, alignment will be achieved. This is Secret #2.

The IT department is a major line item in most corporations. As a percent of revenue, IT costs can be as low as 2 percent and as high at 50 percent in some high-tech businesses. This significant cost expenditure requires some commitment on the part of the corporate officers. It is fashionable for some officers to give IT short shrift either because they have had bad experiences and don't trust IT or they are unsure of themselves in the high-tech arena. Either excuse is a poor one. It is understood that all officers need to be conversant with the sales plan, the marketing plan, and the financial statements. The same should be true of the automation agenda. It is too expensive and it is too risky to delegate it to the IT department.

Before we get into the details of the operations of the steering committee, let's review some alternatives to such a system. For the readers without a committee, one of these should sound familiar:

1. **The Squeaky Wheel.** This method of prioritizing is fraught with problems. It is usually evidenced by an officer or senior manager stopping by the CIO's office and outlining the dire consequences that will befall the company unless IT drops everything and develops a new system. This can be especially intimidating if the complainer outranks the CIO and the CIO has further aspirations in the

company. In companies where this is the rule, the IT department often jumps from project to project based on the clout of the complainer.

2. **The All-Knowing CIO.** This method is often the result of management refusing to participate in the IT prioritization process; or it can be in a situation where the CIO thinks that his/her ideas are the only ones that are valid. Either way, this is a prescription for non-alignment unless the CIO is a god who can always anticipate the needs of the corporation. It also usually results in a short career for the CIO since the CIO must make unilateral decisions determining which systems are important. If the decisions are ever wrong, then the CIO is undoubtedly the one to blame. In addition, the CIO runs the risk of upsetting a powerful executive whose system request wasn't included in the IT plan.

3. **The All-Knowing CEO/COO.** This can be just as dangerous as the all-knowing CIO since the CEO/COO doesn't always have the pulse of all of the departments and may not understand some new initiatives. This is a case where a single point of view could be less effective than a consensus of the officers. However, this is better for the career aspi-

rations of the CIO since it is the boss who is setting the direction.

4. **The Department Heads.** Many companies feel that this process should be delegated one step down in the organization. This could be because the officers have more important things to do, they are uncomfortable with technology discussions, or they feel that it is good training for their subordinates. Despite the urge to remove one responsibility from their plates, it is a bad decision. Suppose a director type decides in the meeting that the project being discussed is more important than his/her project and agrees to delay or cancel it. This is the type of decision that the committee is supposed to make. This can be very problematic to the department head's boss, who was counting on the project to make budget numbers and to expedite the department's agenda.

During my career as a CIO, I never once had to answer an irate user as to why IT was not working on a particular system. Hopefully, this was because all users understood that I did not make that decision. If a particular system needed to be done, then that person should make his/her case to the appropriate officer and bring the case to the steering committee.

Now let's talk about the nuts and bolts of the committee. There are many ways to structure the process. That is not an issue. At the end of the day, if the corporate officers are deciding on the final automation agenda based on the strategic business plans of the company, then the systems will be effective, and the IT agenda will be aligned.

The first step is to decide who should serve as the members of the committee. Minimally, the committee should be composed of the CEO and all of his/her direct reports. Then, if the CIO is not a direct report, he/she should be added. Then I would recommend that any other officers who do not report directly to the CEO should be added. These additional officers are only necessary in the annual prioritization meeting since they might have a better understanding of the new systems being proposed.

Once the membership is finalized, the CIO should decide on some of the processes, such as: when should the group meet, how often, how should the information for decisions be prepared, and what should be the agenda? As I mentioned, there can be much variation in this process. For example, some CIOs like to have a meeting on a semi-annual or even a quarterly basis. This can be helpful if the company is experiencing a great deal of change, causing priorities to be very fluid. My committee, however, would meet for a prioritization session late in the year after the budgets had been submitted but before they had been finalized. In this meeting a subgroup would present a list of the projects to the officers that they felt should be approved for the upcoming year. This list would be based on strategic importance, return on investment (ROI), risk factors, and other issues such as legal or regulatory requirements.

The plan submitted to the officers would show the projects that the subgroup recommends for funding using the budgeted staff resources. The group would also recommend additional projects that the committee felt should be included but could not due to current budgeted strength. The committee would then review all of the funded projects and ask questions about their importance. It is essential that most of these questions be directed to the appropriate officer and not to IT. Of course, technical questions such as impact on the corporate data center or requirement for additional support software would be appropriately directed to IT.

Interestingly, when we first set up this system, some of the officers were not prepared to answer the questions posed, such as, "Why do you need this system?" Often, the system would be dropped from the list if a good case could not be made for the new system. In subsequent meetings, everyone came prepared to defend their request for IT resources.

Next, the committee would review the "want list" and ask the same questions as were asked for the funded projects. The committee would then make several decisions. They could add projects to the funded list, remove some, or even add some that weren't on either list. Once the new funded list was completed, the committee would authorize IT to add staff, hire outside consultants, or buy outside packages. IT would then make the appropriate adjustments to their submitted budget; or, in a charge-out environment, the users would do that.

The committee would review this project list on an ongoing basis throughout the year as business requirements changed, or to update it on the progress of critical items. In addition, the committee would discuss other IT issues including security or response time concerns, or anything else affecting the corporation. At the end of this process, all of the officers would feel involved in the process, would understand what progress was being made, and would have developed a strategic understanding of the IT agenda. Most importantly, this process would assure that IT and the corporation would be aligned.

An example of how the numbers work in the Steering Committee meeting is included in Appendix B.

In Appendix C, you'll find an outline of an actual project that was presented to the IT Steering Committee. This was a very interesting project because it utilized new technologies, had a very large ROI, and was supported by IT, but was not supported by the users. It provides an interesting scenario that asks the question of whether or not IT should push a new technology despite the desires of the user department. Since it is a real case, it will be interesting to hear the opinion of our readers.

CHAPTER 4

Long-Range Planning

Why should involvement in long-range planning be a requirement for a great IT department? Well, the reasons are simple. I cannot imagine a strategic business plan in the modern corporation that doesn't have a major IT component. But at the same time, I can't imagine one without a significant financial, marketing, or manufacturing component. In fact, I feel that there is no such thing as an IT strategic plan any more than there should be a strategic marketing/financial/manufacturing plan. There should be an overall company strategic business plan that requires each department to develop its own tactical plan to accomplish the objectives of the strategic plan. Thus, all major departments should participate in the development of the plan. This is Secret #3.

Let me give you an example. In the late '50s, American Airlines decided to implement the Sabre online reservation system. For its time, it was certainly a massive undertaking for its IT department. But, I would argue that it was just as daunting for all the departments within American, including finance, which would have to develop a new pricing model; marketing, which would have to develop a new go-to-market model; and operations, which would have to develop new algorithms to allocate and fill seats. To my way of thinking, there was only one strategy: Implement Sabre. Each department in American, including IT, developed tactical plans to achieve its business strategy.

However, what happens in many cases is that various executives develop the plans without any input from IT. This happens in companies that look upon IT as a utility that can expand or contract by any amount to fulfill the needs of the corporation. This is a bad mistake. It is very critical that IT is aware of long-term directions so that it can plan for staffing, computer power, storage, and potential new applications that are being considered.

However, IT has an even more important role to play in the planning process. IT must be responsible for staying up to date with new technologies that have the potential to change the company in dramatic and important ways.

As an example: It is said that electronic books already exceed printed books sold by Amazon. I don't exactly know the role that IT played within Borders Books, but I do not think that they had focused on the threat coming from on-line booksellers. If they had been concerned, they would not have outsourced their Web site to their most dangerous competitor, Amazon. Nevertheless, they were late to the party relative to electronic readers that are taking over the market.

New technologies are emerging very rapidly (How many people heard about electronic readers before they were present and rapidly emerging in the market?), and they need to be carefully considered by a company before they are used by other companies to take market share and destroy firms such as Borders. I would argue that a rigorous long-range planning process—which addresses strengths, weaknesses, threats, and opportunities—would have identified this threat before it became critical. And if the process included all corporate officers including those from IT, there would have been a good chance to head it off or, at least, reduce its internal impact.

Certainly, IT should not be the only area of the company that keeps its eye on technology. Developments in advanced robotics, the mapping of the human genome, nanotechnology, and rapidly increasing computer power have the potential of significantly changing the way companies do business in the very near future.

Ray Kurzweil, the author of *The Singularity Is Near: When Humans Transcend Biology*, argues the case very persuasively: technology will be instrumental in significantly increasing human life spans by reducing the impact of serious disease. He also feels that robotics will significantly change the manufacturing tradeoffs even more significantly than they already have. He argues that advanced nanotechnology will result in a renaissance in the way all businesses approach their markets. Thus, I would say that the whole company must become digitally savvy, and it should become routine to talk about these developments in the long-range planning process. However, it must fall to IT to be the instrument of this discussion and bring to the table some of the newest and most promising endeavors.

In the companies with great IT organizations, IT participates in the process that results in the long-range plan. Once the plan is finalized, the rest of the company works with its IT representatives to develop their IT requirements based on that plan. Then the plan is submitted to the sub-group that develops a preliminary plan based on that long-range plan. This preliminary plan is then submitted to the IT Steering Committee.

CHAPTER 5

A Defined System Development Process

As the title of this book indicates, there are 9 1/2 secrets of a great IT organization. A major element of the 9 1/2 secrets is the requirement to have user involvement in all of them. As we've already discussed, it is certainly necessary for the CEO to be involved in the reporting relationship of IT. It is also essential that the CEO and officer group understand and participate in the proper functioning of the IT steering committee. In addition, it is critical that all participating users understand the role of IT in the long-range planning process.

The first three secrets require user involvement at the highest levels of the company. The fourth secret requires participation from users throughout the corporation. In addition, this secret involves some of the most intense work necessary in order to have a great IT organization.

Using a defined system development process should begin when a project has been approved by the IT Steering Committee and is given a start date by IT. The project start date is when the first meeting between IT and the user of the new system takes place—beginning a relationship that will exist through system implementation. User involvement will vary throughout the process but this project must remain a high priority for them.

Perhaps, as a user, you are saying at this point, "Why do I have to be involved in this process? I have enough to do, and this is IT's job." This relates back to the comment made in chapter 3. At the end of the process the user will own the system, not IT. This is somewhat different than the other departments within the company. If the advertising department gets approval from management to develop a new advertising plan, it is the responsibility of advertising to find an ad agency, define the parameters of the campaign, and manage a selection process designed to pick the most effective execution of the desired message. Perhaps the officers and staff will be brought in toward the end of the process to offer their opinions but, at the end of the day, the responsibility for the success or failure of the campaign rests on the back of the advertising department.

If the strategic plan calls for a new manufacturing process, it is the responsibility of that department to engineer the new process, spec the machining requirements, put the development out to bid, and implement the new process. Certainly, throughout that process there would be status updates for the company management, but ultimately the responsibility for the success or failure of the system resides with manufacturing management.

When it comes to an IT project, many users probably think that they should operate in the same way, meaning IT develops and then owns this new system. Most users don't—but should—notice a difference. IT is not proposing a new automated system; the user department is. Even so, the users often feel that their role is merely to provide a bare bones description of the problem the system will be designed to resolve, and to let IT take it from there by developing a technology based solution.

Many users feel that it is IT's job to divine what the users want and deliver a completed system to them with a minimum of user involvement. It would be no different than advertising management hiring an agency and giving them minimal direction about their ideas and letting them come up with the final campaign without involvement from the user; or, the manufacturing department letting an outside engineering company take over their plant to implement a proposed system for fulfilling their manufacturing needs with minimal involvement from the users.

Most of us would say that either of these scenarios would never happen. Why then do some users abdicate this responsibility when it comes to IT systems? IT systems will oftentimes run an aspect of the department and have the potential of having a bigger impact on the company than the manufacturing or advertising examples described earlier in this chapter.

The reasons this lack of participation is more apt to happen with an IT project is because users have very little awareness of the importance of the process, and because IT has done a very poor job explaining to the user the importance of the process. Users feel that this is IT's job, even though they would never leave an almost identical process to the ad agency or the engineering firm.

IT, on the other hand, may not call for user involvement. They may be content in making their own decisions since users will often not be able to make up their minds as to how a system should work. Thus, it is easier to not ask the users and just do it the way that IT thinks is best. This is very dangerous and can lead to user dissatisfaction with the resulting system and a lot of costly rework.

Another not so obvious reason for the lack of user involvement is the general perception of IT and of IT professionals. Most users are not comfortable interfacing with IT professionals and some IT professionals don't do much to assist users in overcoming the perception that they are difficult to work with, don't understand the business, and don't speak the user's language. Add all this to the need for an IT defined development process and you have one large wall to break through. All this does not make it very easy for IT to get user involvement no matter how well defined the methodology. Nonetheless, a well-documented, management supported development process is essential for a viable and successful IT department.

So, the best way to ensure the users will participate is to require their participation by means of a standardized process. Several Systems Development Life Cycles (SDLCs) or software development processes have been used to ensure the successful development of IT solutions. SDLC models can be described along the spectrum from agile to iterative to sequential, and they are all structured approaches for developing, maintaining, and replacing information systems.

The most common SDLCs have five phases. They are planning, analysis, design, implementation, and maintenance. Each phase will require various levels of user involvement. Recently, Agile methodologies, such as XP and Scrum, have become very popular within IT organizations. These methods are lightweight, iterative processes allowing for rapid changes along the development cycle and promise to shorten the time needed to complete a project but require a heavier commitment on the part of the user. There are many variations of these methodologies, including prototyping and rapid application development (RAD) among others.

Just as important as obtaining user and IT involvement is documenting the process to avoid any misunderstandings during system development and to ensure all deliverables and milestones are met and approved for each phase. This avoids being 90 percent completed and way off track before anyone realizes what has gone wrong.

Another factor to consider is that if the user does not have the time or the staff to participate as required to ensure a successful implementation, the project should be put on hold and IT resources be redeployed to another project where user support can be provided. Unfortunately, what usually happens when users do not participate is that IT assumes the full burden of completing the project, making the best decisions they can. This almost guarantees costly rework.

I have one final comment about this process. Regardless of the methodology that is used to manage and complete the project, there is a phase that is seldom done but should be done in a great IT organization. The mysteriously missing phase is the post-implementation review. Because it is seldom utilized as a phase in the development process, it has been included here as a 1/2 secret, thus the 9 **1/2** secrets.

The final step should be to analyze and assess the success of the project. It is rarely done because it needs to be scheduled, at minimum, one year after the system is implemented. This is because the full benefit of the system cannot be recognized immediately after it goes live. It usually takes at least a year for all benefits of the system to be realized. After one year, it is very hard to get the people that worked on the system back together. Most have probably moved on to other assignments or may have left the company. In addition, user management and IT management will not be interested in diverting resources to this less than profit making venture. Also, no one is very interested in such work either from the IT side or the user side.

Having said that, I would still argue that it is a very important phase and some companies, like Intel, do a very good job with it. The main reason to conduct such an audit is to verify that the results that were expected when the project was approved by the Steering Committee have been met:

- Was the project successful in solving the problem outlined by the user?

- Was it done on time and within budget?

- If not, did the project experience new requests by the users that expanded the initial concept?

- Was the initial ROI achieved? If not, why not?

- Will user management achieve any expected decrease in headcount?

- What about any promised sales increases or other cost reductions?

Answering these questions serves two purposes. The first one is to determine the accuracy of the ROIs that the users submitted to justify the development of the system. If these ROIs are never verified, there is no way to control their size in the future. If users discover that large ROIs have a better chance of approval, they will start to exaggerate them.

The other very important reason to conduct these audits is to answer the question, "What is the value of IT?" The CEO or other officers are inclined to ask this question at least once a year during budget season. Executives look at IT's high expenses and wonder if they are getting enough results from IT to justify the cost. IT usually has little empirical data to answer the question since IT development and operation is a cost. The cost savings or sales increases resulting from new computer systems always flow into the budgets of the user department, and very few of the benefits flow to IT. In fact, most user managers fail to attribute their success in increasing revenue or reducing cost to IT. In these cases, the cause is usually "good management." In addition, most managers do not like being held to headcount reductions. They would rather redeploy resources that have been freed up due to new systems.

The solution to this dilemma is to have the work done by an audit function outside of the IT or user department. I would recommend that the finance department do it, especially if they already have an audit function. This group could be involved throughout the project so that there is some awareness of the project and its proposed benefits. At the end of this phase, the company would be aware of the success of the project, the accuracy of the projection, and the contribution of IT.

CHAPTER 6

Up-to-Date Hardware and Software

There are many reasons to maintain an up-to-date hardware and software environment in today's modern corporation. The number one reason is to achieve the full capability of computer systems. Out-of-date hardware is often too slow to use the latest software, while out-of-date software is usually not fully supported and could result in major problems should vendor support be required. This is Secret #5.

There is no doubt that the ongoing requirement to upgrade is a source of angst within most companies since they continually see computer costs escalating. However, executives must realize that it is no different than keeping your car and truck fleets up to date, or assuring that your insurance is the best possible, or that the latest products are being sold. It sometimes seems like executives feel that they are buying their last computer when they make a big commitment to hardware only to find out that their purchase was probably obsolete the day it arrived.

When we started in computers, there were no PCs. Terminals only existed on the largest mainframe computers, and only data (numbers and letters) were depicted on the screens. Today we have real-time full motion video in full color along with any type of interactive process that one can imagine; and experts say that this speedy evolution of technology will continue at an even more rapid pace. It is extremely dangerous to let your software and hardware inventory become outdated. This can only open the way for competitors to gain a competitive advantage by more fully utilizing the capabilities that accrue to early adopters or even normal adopters.

The second reason for keeping up to date is the effect on staff. People in IT are interested in using the latest tools and equipment to enable them to accomplish their jobs in a quicker and more efficient manner. No one wants to work on old equipment that is more difficult to work with when there are better alternatives. It is no different than having employees work in old-fashioned environments with outdated equipment, or having salesmen driving old cars or manufacturers using outdated techniques. Everyone wants to work with the latest equipment.

However, there is a caveat to this. IT should never recommend new software or hardware just for the sake of having new hardware or software. The decision to upgrade should only be made when there is a good business reason, such as: additional capabilities, avoidance of increased support charges, or a decrease in development time. Technology for "technology's sake" is not a sufficient reason to upgrade.

It is also important for companies to display an up-to-date working environment to attract the best people possible. There are many reasons the top talent pick a company. You don't want an outdated environment to cause a good prospective employee to say no.

This is a good place to talk about the cost of IT. IT has a great deal of discretion regarding its spending levels. There are fixed costs that are hard to control. There is a certain amount of money needed to run the current production environment. There is a base of systems that must be run in order for the company to operate.

As an alternative, there is the possibility of outsourcing this to an outside data center rather than running the work on company owned equipment. Many companies are providing this service, and it can be a way to reduce costs. Be careful that the company providing the service is safe, is also protected from disaster, and can move quickly should problems occur. Remember, internal computer systems are the lifeblood of the company. Also, once you have moved all of your processing offsite and eliminated your data center, it is very difficult to reverse direction and reinstitute the center. Usually, staff has moved on and the technology has probably changed.

A trend that is on the increase is using the cloud to run systems on a vendor's computer rather than one owned or outsourced by the user. Again, it is important to understand that there are many risks that could befall a company if the outsourcer gets into trouble. This requires a lot of oversight by the user and it is difficult to reverse. However, it can be a way to reduce costs in IT.

It is also possible to outsource or offshore much staff work in order to reduce costs. Again, vigilance is important to assure that your data is secure and not being misused by the outsourcer. It is also critical to maintain a certain level of knowledge on the internal staff. Remember, the people in IT are probably the only people in the company who really know the details of how things work deep in the bowels of the computer systems. In addition to using some of these new ways to reduce costs, IT must also consider response time requirements. If the company is willing to endure longer response times, there are ways to reduce hardware costs to achieve that.

Suffice it to say, there are many ways to control costs but it must be consistent with the need to provide the expected level of service to the users and protect the integrity of the company's information.

CHAPTER 7

Commitment to Training

If I were an aspiring IT worker interviewing for a new position today, the first question I would ask my prospective new employer would be about the company training program. The reason is simple, the IT industry changes technology as quickly as any industry around today. What is current one year is passé the next. This "ever-changeability" is part of the reason why users have a hard time understanding the typical IT practitioner because technological terms and jargon are always in a state of flux.

Despite its effect on the user community, language reflects the "state of the art." Technology tradeoffs are changing every day as cost benefit calculations spike to ever-higher levels. The only way to keep ahead of the curve is to be sure that the internal IT department is up to date with what is going on in the industry. This is Secret #6.

Staying up to date begins with the CIO and travels down throughout the organization. New technologies should be routinely discussed in staff meetings so everyone is apprised of the latest advancements and how these changes could be used to help the company. This type of discussion will migrate down the organization and move into the user community when discussions about the future begin in earnest prior to the IT Steering Committee selection meeting.

This will also signal to the entire organization that IT is constantly learning and keeping abreast of the latest and greatest developments to ensure the company stays competitive. In my experience, it is sometimes IT personnel who are the most change-resistant people in the organization. "If it works, don't fix it," is their mantra and is probably a learned behavior from their early days in IT, when they were never sure exactly why some of our changes were actually working. In order to offset this type of thinking, an organization must require that the staff be exposed to outside seminars, participate in local and national user groups, and stay conversant with the major trends affecting the industry.

Having a structured training program is critical to the success of a great IT organization. The program is an indication to staff members that the company is concerned about their professional and personal growth, and wants to ensure they are able to perform to their full potential. An integral part of the training program should be a skills assessment. Everyone should be required to complete one. This assessment will be used to determine skill levels to ensure they match those required for current positions. If not, the assessment should highlight those areas requiring training and recommend specific courses. The assessment can also be used to prepare staff for promotion. In this case, courses are recommended to bring the individual up to the skill level required of the new position.

Companies must be aware that there are many available types of training, delivered in numerous ways. Let's first talk about conferences. I would say that, unfortunately, many companies use attendance at these conferences (there are plenty) as a benefit for those that are in favor at the present time. This is okay in some cases because those in favor are often the ones doing the best work. However, these conferences are quite beneficial and most definitely should be used to broaden one's view and enable everyone in the department to grow professionally and personally. This is where new ideas come from.

I would also require that conference attendees write a report when they return to the office, outlining what they learned and how it could apply to the company. My direction was to get at least one idea from each session whether it was plenary or a breakout. I would often take these reports, discuss them internally, and then discuss some of the highlights with the officer group or even to the Board of Directors.

The next area is technical training. This type of training can be delivered in a live seminar, either in house or as a public workshop, video based or as e-learning. I once talked to a CIO from a major Fortune 500 company who boasted that he would routinely use consultants to do the new, innovative work and let his internal staff work on the more mundane enhancement work. He said that it showed his staff that they weren't as smart as they thought that they were. Guess what? The staff figured it out relatively quickly and they realized that the "fun" work was being done at the consultancies and it was time to get out the resume.

I approached this issue a little bit differently. I assumed that IT professionals were all smart people and had been attracted to IT because of the challenge. While it is true that you probably need some outside assistance when a new technology is initially chosen, it should be your goal to train your staff in the new technology and replace the outside consultants as soon as possible. The internal staff really appreciates the opportunity and feels that they are moving forward in the corporation. Of course, that makes your staff more marketable, but that is a good problem because you are raising their skill level. It's your job to continually challenge them and make them feel comfortable and appreciated. Then, if there was difficulty completing all of the work, consultants could be hired to complete the uninteresting aspects of the project. Remember, consultants will do anything for a fee.

Another strategic aspect of the training program should be to predict future technologies and to get the staff trained prior to the actual need. This is tricky since you don't want to train someone in a technology and then have a period of time when they cannot use the skills that they have learned. The closer you can get the training to the need the better, and the less you will have to pay for high-priced consultants. This is known as "just-in-time training" and has been used effectively by many great IT organizations.

It is also a good thing to remember that technical training is not just about the newest and greatest technologies. Technical training must also include training in the project management and project analysis skills that are needed to bring projects in on time and under budget. Sometimes, IT can piggyback on corporate training that is already being done in these areas since these skills are usually needed across the corporation.

Finally, there is management training. IT has been lax over the years in training promising managers in the skills needed to change from a technologist to a manager. This transition is especially difficult for technical people who are used to controlling every aspect of their work since they know that any little innocuous error could affect the entire project. Therefore, it is necessary for the CIO to identify those people who are management material and give them some skills so that they are more apt to succeed in this new world of management. Many times technologists are unsure of this career change and would have to be convinced that such a change is good for them and the company.

We will talk more about this situation in the next chapter.

CHAPTER 8

Dual Career Paths

Without a doubt, the most important asset in the IT department goes out the door every evening and, hopefully, returns every morning. In all modern-day corporations, the company infrastructure is run by the IT department; how it all works and comes together is unknown by most senior managers. I remember one time taking a senior executive in my firm on a tour of our data center. At the end of the tour, it was obvious by his questions that he was very impressed. As he departed, he smiled and told me that it would never work!

Yet, day in and day out, the computers run; the systems pass data from one system to another; the reports that are sent across the corporation are printed; managers make decisions based on data presented on screens; and new systems are proposed, developed, and implemented. The systems work. But, who makes them work? This task falls on the backs of the technology professionals who are generally unknown to the majority of the corporation. These are the developers, systems analysts, network specialists, Web site integrators, security specialists, system software technicians, and many other people with unknown job titles that make it all work. In earlier, simpler days, the company had departments that used paper and pencil to develop the information that ran the company. Today, this information comes from computer systems and few people have any idea who is doing the work, what they are doing, or how the work is done.

Because of this transfer of responsibility from the user department to the IT department, it is critical that IT nurtures and maintains a competent and knowledgeable workforce that maintains the integrity of the systems and assures that they are producing accurate and reliable data. These are highly skilled jobs that are staffed by a workforce that is young and highly mobile, especially in good economic times. Typically, most of the jobs are not industry dependent.

For example, a network specialist or a system designer can work for a manufacturer, a retailer, an insurance company, or a consulting firm. The work is somewhat the same and the employee can easily adapt to new environments. In essence, the competition for these people comes from the entire market, including the public and private sectors.

Thus, the need to develop an environment that will enable these professionals to achieve their personal objectives is very important. As I mentioned in the last chapter, there is a need to identify some of the staff as potential management candidates and train them in the technical skills and human relations skills that will enable them to become project leaders, project managers and maybe even the CIO.

It must be understood that it is just as important to create an environment in which the technical employee can thrive and prosper. IT, like other technical professions, often attracts people who have no interest in managing others but are very good at making sure that the systems and computers run as effectively as possible.

These "super techs" want to see that their technical skills are appreciated by the company, and they want to know they have a career growth path. They are concerned that this may not be the case because they often see the management track as the only way to get better promotions, raises, and recognition.

Just as in sports, it should be possible and not be considered an anomaly when a manager is paid less than a subordinate. The company should understand that both skills are critical for success, and the jobs should be paid based on what the market dictates, not what the internal compensation plan dictates. This is Secret #7.

I remember in the early days of my career, we brought in a developer that had the reputation of being a "super coder." As I remember, he was a less than remarkable character. He wore a rumpled suit and a white shirt and a narrow black tie. In fact, every day that I saw him, he had on the exact same outfit. I just hoped he changed his shirt at least occasionally. He didn't talk much, but his output was prodigious. He worked very strange hours. He would roll in about 10:00 a.m. but would work all night long; and I never even saw him eat anything. He was totally enraptured by the technology and probably produced five times more work than any mere mortal. People like this were, and are, vitally important to the IT department and need to be recognized for their superior efforts.

The modern IT department needs to have people who are outgoing, business savvy, people oriented, and tactful. From this pool, potential managers must be identified. The department also needs people who have no interest in interacting with users or managing others but would rather work on system problems and develop solutions that serve the users in a different non-personal manner. Both are vital to the success of the modern IT organization.

CHAPTER 9

Disaster Recovery Planning

When I was a CIO, people would ask me, "What keeps you awake at night?" and I would always answer, "A system security breach." I believe that most senior corporate executives would answer the same way if they only understood the risks inherent in today's computer systems.

Making disaster recovery planning a high priority for IT is Secret #8.

However, the opposite is true in most companies and in most IT organizations. The CIO designates someone or some group to handle the security requirements of the corporate systems, and then goes on to other things, assuming those issues are being handled. Most CIOs have, at best, a passing knowledge of the intricacies of maintaining a robust and effective system security defense.

Before we delve into the new struggles involved in maintaining strong system security bulwarks, let's discuss two other system dangers that have been around for a long time. The first is natural or man-made disasters. Hurricanes, floods, fires, tornadoes, terrorist attacks, and other calamities head the list of potential risks to corporate systems.

Most of the time, we read little of these events due to the very real concern of the impact to corporate reputation, market share, and stock price. I remember reading about several IT departments that performed heroic deeds in their efforts to reestablish computing in their companies after 9/11. But, such stories are rare. This must have been the case after the devastation caused by Hurricane Katrina or in the Midwest during outbreaks of tornadoes.

There are several alternatives available to address this issue:

- Subscribing to a third-party off-site computer room called a hot site.

- Arranging a mutual aid pact with another company.

- Installing redundant equipment at alternate locations.

- Moving all critical applications to the cloud.

There are pros and cons for each of these methods. The hot site is a good solution, but can be difficult to start up, can be somewhat expensive, and could be problematic to use in the case of a widespread disaster like a flood. The mutual pact is great in concept, but very difficult in practice. It can be hard to arrange testing and, if needed, can cause the company without a disaster to have one of their own. Redundant computers, especially ones that are in different locations, are an ideal solution but are the most expensive alternative. It allows ease of testing, and the company controls access and capacity. The cloud promises an effective solution, but vigilance is important to assure that the computer locations in the cloud are also safe from disasters.

In all of these cases, it is important to remember that testing the efficacy of the method chosen is critical to its success during an actual disaster. Based on the option selected, this process can involve varying degrees of difficulty. The cloud needs the least amount of testing, and the mutual aid pact the most due to the ever-changing environment of an active data center. The other caveat is that the users must be heavily involved in the process to assure that the most important applications get the highest priority. A triage system must be proposed and agreed to by the users, and it must be adhered to in the disaster scenario.

The second non-system security risk is a system bug that could bring down the system. This type of problem can be very traumatic since it requires IT to drop everything and fix it immediately. This sometimes involves telephone calls in the dead of night or contacting people on vacation. However, once the proper person is contacted, the problem is usually solvable by the IT department.

Despite the fact that a non-functioning program can cause very critical outages that can be devastating to the company, there usually aren't long-term issues. This, of course, can be a very different story in super critical applications such as law enforcement, space travel, or critical infrastructure. It can also be more long term if the proper people cannot be found to handle the problem, or if the issue is more structural or logic based. Nevertheless, this type of outage is generally not as critical as a natural disaster or a security breach would be.

Now let's turn to the security breach. As I mentioned, there is an overall lack of awareness of this problem and a lack of understanding of its potential impact. This type of breach has the potential of destroying a company. In the early days of hacking, there were many people trying to penetrate system security and doing minimal damage. The challenge was the conquest of the security defense. Many of these offenses received a lot of press but there was very little lasting damage.

More recently, this problem has become more virulent. There have been successful security breaches resulting in the theft of credit card information, attempts to penetrate defense systems, attempts to steal corporate secrets, or just to bring the company down. There is no question that the hacker community is getting more sophisticated and the potential damage to target corporations is much greater. This problem has also been elevated to the state level where cyber warfare has already begun and could become the weapon of choice in the future.

Many companies have identified this risk and have established high-level security departments, oftentimes positioned at the officer level. Others have kept their heads in the sand and just hoped that nothing bad will happen. It is incumbent upon all CIOs who want to have a great IT organization to get involved in system security.

I have several recommendations in this area. The CIO should have a regular quarterly meeting with the security staff to better understand their issues and to assist in providing the needed resources. The CIO should occasionally attend security conferences with the security staff in order to understand the current threats that could have a negative effect on the corporation. I also feel that this issue should be brought to the Board level so that the board members understand the risks and understand what is being done to ensure the safety of the system.

Finally, I would encourage an ongoing security audit by a trusted outside firm that would give a second opinion on the safety of the current system environment and also write a report outlining additional steps that need to be taken. This advisor could also keep the company informed on the latest threats and the methods required to provide protection. They could also become advisors to the Board, not unlike the outside auditors employed by all companies to protect against financial problems and misrepresentations.

Disaster recovery planning is a potential high-risk area for the IT department and the company. It is the responsibility of IT to protect the integrity of the systems. It is one area that companies cannot afford to shortchange. Besides, IT people like to get a good night's sleep.

CHAPTER 10

Status and
Metrics Reporting

Many users feel that the IT department is a black hole that things go into but never come out of. Substantiating that perception are the many IT departments that like it that way and believe that the less scrutiny, the better. That is very dangerous for the modern IT organization. If IT wants to be a great enigma, then it should be willing to accept the consequences that follow. This mentality justifies receiving a lack of respect, mistrust of intent, and difficulty in entering into the mainstream of the company. Instead, IT must try to open itself up, show itself off and be accountable for its actions. IT must be equally willing to accept praise when it is successful and accept blame when it is at fault. In short, IT must start acting like other departments in the company.

The best way to eliminate this veil of secrecy that has fallen over most IT activities is to develop a reporting methodology that communicates the status of projects to everyone in the corporation. This is Secret #9.

In my company, we published a report every month listing the projects that were approved, those that were completed, those in process, and those yet to be started. In addition, we included the original cost estimate for each project, an estimated completion date (if in process), and any changes that caused these initial estimates to be adjusted. We then justified any variations from the original estimates by indicating errors by IT in the initial estimate, new requests by the users (sometimes called scope creep), or new findings during development that changed the estimate.

We then published this report on the corporate Intranet for everyone to see. We highlighted every major change in yellow so no one could miss it. Any major changes would be discussed in detail at the next officers' meeting. This way there were no surprises on major projects, and the officer group could discuss any ramifications that may occur due to the delay of any major implementations. As a result, discussions of IT progress became a routine part of everyday business. In addition, users across the company became very familiar with the major projects and their status. No one could ever say that they were blindsided by delays in project completion.

We did something else that enabled us to be more successful in meeting deadlines and budgets. We began to pay IT practitioners an incentive if they were successful in completing projects on time and within budget. It was amazing how this small step got projects done on time, eliminated a lot of scope creep requests from the users, required fewer changes in each monthly report, and began to give IT a better reputation on getting the job done.

This report was also the basis for each IT Steering Committee meeting that we held throughout the year to discuss status of projects. Based on issues, we would hold such a meeting quarterly or more often as needs required. At these interim meetings, we would discuss project progress, any significant cost issues raised by the new projects, and any other IT issues that rose to the level of the officers' concerns.

At some meetings, we were required to modify the project prioritization due to a change in the business, government requirements, legal issues, or changes in in-process projects that had the potential of significantly changing the ROI. This could be caused by changes by an outside vendor, requirement changes by the user that would significantly change the deliverables of the project, technical problems found during development, or any of a myriad of other issues that affected the completion and/or the cost of the project.

This process also kept the officer group engaged in the IT agenda and partly responsible for its actions. Since users ultimately own the IT projects, this is the proper way to do it in the modern corporation.

Metrics are also an important step in the maturation of any IT department. Numbers are the language of business, and knowledgeable executives always know the key numbers that are critical for the company. However, there are many IT executives who speak in generalities about their department, and really haven't tried to document the critical numbers that should point out to others the successes of the IT department.

IT leaders should:

- Know the average response time for critical online systems.

- Know the mean time to resolve any online problems for users.

- Track disk utilization and processor utilization on the mainframe/servers in order to anticipate upgrades.

- Be aware of the cost of IT as a percentage of revenue, and they should be able to talk to their CEOs about the return on investment that IT has achieved over the past year.

- Be aware of how much enhancement/maintenance work the department does relative to new development, and also be aware of the size of their actual and potential development backlog.

Suffice it to say, a CIO who can quantify his/her operation in business measurement terms has a much better chance of being accepted by the company establishment that thrives on this kind of information. It will make IT look much more like an actual department rather than a group that relates more to its technology than to the corporation.

CHAPTER 11

The Digitally Aligned Corporation

As mentioned in the Foreword, the major objective of this book is to explain the 9 1/2 steps that will assist in creating an IT department that is aligned with the goals of the corporation.

One of the things I wanted to stress in this chapter is the role of the user in each of the steps. This is probably the most important aspect of the 9 1/2 secrets—each has a user component that must be implemented in order for the IT department to be successful.

It is the CEO, the ultimate user, who must understand the unique role of IT in the modern corporation and be wise

enough to understand why IT should be reporting directly to his/her level. It is the corporate officers who must
see the need to participate in the IT Steering Committee
to ensure that the systems needed by the corporation to
achieve their goals are being developed. They must also
see the need to include IT in the long-range planning
process, to assure that IT has the resources to execute the
plan, and that IT has a voice in bringing new technological solutions to the table.

It is the company managers who must understand the need
to participate with their staff in the system development
process in order to develop the best possible systems for
the company. It is executive management, especially on the
financial side, that must understand the need to stay up to
date with the latest and most productive technologies. It is
the human resources department that must understand the
need to provide training, even if it is significantly more than
the amount of training given to other departments. They
must also work with IT to create their dual career paths
in order to award the high achievers on both the technical
and management sides. This includes salary levels, titles,
and perks that may be different from other departments.

The entire company must understand the potential dangers that exist with physical or system security outages.
They must all be willing to participate with IT in practic-

ing disaster recovery drills and be as prepared as possible for the worst-case scenario. They must also be willing to read the monthly status reports so that they understand the implications of changing specifications and try to minimize them in order to complete as many critical projects as possible.

Finally, management of the company must understand the need to do the post-development reviews so that the company can fully understand the true role that IT plays in managing the costs and increasing the sales of the corporation. In this way, IT can take its proper place as a very important cog in the corporate wheel, rather than be a player in the love-hate relationship that is sometimes experienced.

Having the users involved with the implementation of every secret will probably be the hardest part to achieve. IT can want to do things, but it must have the necessary user support. IT must nurture these relationships, it must show its true professionalism by getting the work done, and it must convince the users that they have to learn and understand the true role of IT in the modern corporation. This is where the rubber meets the road and is the biggest challenge for today's CIO.

I hope that you have found the 9 1/2 secrets to be realistic and, at the same time, challenging for some corporate cultures. If that is true, then the book has achieved its objective. Please take a minute to complete the scorecard in Appendix A to rate your IT department and then develop a plan to improve its execution.

Appendices

Appendix A:
The 9 1/2 Secrets Scorecard

Appendix B:
Company XYZ IT
Steering Committee

Appendix C:
Catalog Automation Case Study

APPENDIX A

The 9 1/2 Secrets Scorecard

Use this appendix to rate an IT department and determine whether or not it is "great." A perfect score is 95. Once you've completed your assessment, you can ascertain how far the department is from the ideal. I have intentionally not suggested how much to subtract from the points in each category. I'll leave it up to you to determine the extent to which the firm being evaluated follows or doesn't follow the recommended methodology.

Secret #1:
The CIO Should Report Directly to the CEO

Give the department 10 points if the CIO is an officer of the company, and if he/she reports directly to the CEO or COO. Deduct 10 points if he/she reports to any other officer and more if the top IT person is not an officer.

Secret #2:
Having an IT Steering Committee
Composed of Corporate Officers

Give the department 10 points if there is a committee composed of all of the company officers or at least all of the officers reporting to the CEO. Take points away if the committee does not determine the annual IT automation agenda, or if all officers or departments are not represented.

Secret #3:
IT Must Participate in Long-Range Planning

Give the department 10 points if IT fully participates in the planning process. Take points away if IT is involved after the fact or on an as-needed basis. Also take points away if the IT representative is of a lower rank than representatives from other departments.

Secret #4:
Use of Well-Understood System
Development Processes

Give the department 10 points if all major systems are controlled via an approach that is well understood by IT and the users. It makes no difference which approach is used as long as it is well understood. Various outsourcing methods can be used as long as the process is understood. Take points away if this is not done for all systems.

Secret #5:
Use of Up-To-Date Hardware and Software

Give the department 10 points if IT makes every effort to keep up to date with mainframes, servers, PCs, and hand-held devices. It is acceptable to skip a release occasionally for good reason, but this should be done only for good reasons. Take points away if this is not done due to cost savings or because the current system works.

Secret #6:
Commitment to Training

Give the department 10 points if staff routinely attends industry conferences, takes any courses that anticipate new technologies, or attends sessions that will improve their system knowledge. Take points away if training is only allowed as a perk or if there is no attempt to match staff skills with requirements.

Secret #7:
Dual Career Paths

Give the department 10 points if there are technical staff in positions with salaries exceeding those of their manager. Take points away if there is no job description for such a job or only a few token holders of such a position.

Secret #8:
Disaster Recovery Planning is a High Priority for IT

Give the department 10 points if it has a well-organized, influential system security group that is well respected and listened to by the CIO and the entire department. Also, to get this rating, the department must have an organized disaster plan that is tested on a regular basis. Take points away based on your assessment of the commitment to this issue by IT management and the user community.

Secret #9:
Regular Status and Metrics Reporting

Give the department 10 points if it produces, at minimum, a monthly report that shows the status of all approved projects. Take points away if this kind of report is done infrequently or it contains very little status information. Also, to get a 10, the department must have a set of success metrics that show the effectiveness of the operation. Deduct points if these metrics are not routinely updated and utilized.

Secret #9 1/2:
Post Implementation Review

Give the department 5 points if it routinely conducts these reviews on all major projects. Take points away if it is done infrequently or when there are questions raised. Also take points away if the reviews are not quantified in order to determine the effective ROI.

Let me know how the department you are evaluating rates, or if you have any questions. My contact information is in the "Contact Me" section of my Web site, www.paulingevaldson.com.

Good Luck!

APPENDIX B

Company XYZ IT Steering Committee

Project Selection Meeting

Company XYZ has 100 employees working in the IT department. Of these, 25 work in the operations area and are not part of the development team. Of the remaining 75 people in the development area, 6 work in the database area, 5 work in the systems software area, and 8 personnel work in general administration areas. That leaves 56 personnel dedicated to systems development. This calculates to 672 person months per annum. Approximately 15 percent of the available person months are used for administrative reasons such as vacation, training, meetings and other non-development work. That results in 571 months available for development.

Approximately 10 percent of development time must be assumed to be used for technical maintenance. This is work that must be done on existing systems due to errors, changes in software, or other technical reasons. The development subcommittee has thus allocated the remaining 514 person months for the upcoming year. Listed below is the subcommittee's recommendation for the use of these months. Also listed below are the additional projects that the subcommittee feels that the IT steering committee should consider for completion.

Funded projects recommended for approval:

1. Ongoing projects from previous year   150pm

2. Corporate Web Site Development   35pm

3. ERP System Evaluation   125pm

4. Web-Based Personnel System   38pm

5. New Market ID System   87pm

6. User Requested Enhancements   79pm

Unfunded projects recommended for approval:

1. CRM System   100pm

2. Import Management System   25pm

3. Customer Loyalty Program   35pm

Questions for Discussion:

What options does the committee have?

What questions should they ask in the meeting? And of whom?

APPENDIX C

Catalog Automation Case Study

Paul's Hardware in 1980 was a 50 plus-year-old company that operated nine distribution centers across the United States. The company is a dealer-owned cooperative whose mission is to wholesale products to its 4,500 dealer-owners as a way to minimize inventory for the independent retailer at the lowest possible cost.

The catalog department at Paul's Hardware was tasked with the responsibility of keeping the dealer catalogs up to date with any new products, or price or description changes. The catalog was used by the dealers to determine the products available in the warehouse. There were nine versions of this catalog in order to customize the inventory to the area served by the dealer's home distribution center. Each catalog consisted of approximately 1,000 pages and was stored in heavy-duty loose-leaf binders in the stores.

The updating process was very cumbersome. Each page consisted of a listing of the picture, description, and cost information of multiple items carried in the warehouse. When a change was submitted by the buying department, the catalog department used cut-and-paste techniques to update the physical page and send it to the printing department where high-speed web presses were used to print copies and ultimately send the updated pages to the dealer. There was no computerization used in this process.

The CIO at Paul's was aware of this department and the significant cost and time that was needed to keep the catalog updated. However, he knew that he could not automate the process due to the requirement for graphics on the catalog pages. At the time of this case, there were no printers that printed graphics. There were two main choices for high-speed printers in the corporate data center. One was called a line printer that operated at between 600 to 1,200 lines per minute. The technology was similar to a typewriter where a hammer was triggered and it hit the paper through an ink roll. In these data center printers there were multiple sets of characters on a moving chain that enabled the printer to attain this rapid speed.

The second alternative was a laser printer that significantly increased the speed to a rate of two pages per second. The primary supplier of this technology was the Xerox Corporation. However, these printers were very large, occupied a significant footprint in the data center, and could cost upward of $500,000.

These printers were only able to print letters, numbers, or special characters. For years, Paul's Hardware had resisted the laser printers due to their high cost despite the speed advantage of the laser technology. At one point the CIO at Paul's Hardware said to the sales rep, "I can't justify the cost of the laser printer for normal IT reports. However, if you can ever print graphics, I may be interested."

One day, the Xerox representative called on Paul's and said, "We can print graphics. There will be an unveiling of the system in Ottawa, Canada, and you are invited."

Now it was time for the CIO to put up or shut up. IT contacted the user department to see if they would be interested in accompanying them on the trip. There was no interest. This particular application was not a strategic issue for the user department and they were not interested in learning about the new technology. Despite this rebuke, a three-person team, including the CIO, traveled to Ottawa to see the system.

What they saw was very exciting. They had taken two line drawings, one inch by one inch, of a meat grinder and a teakettle that was available from the warehouse. When they arrived at the demonstration site, they were shown a computer that had a laser scanner and a laser printer connected to it as peripheral devices. They placed the picture of the teakettle on the glass of a laser scanner. In those days, such a scanner was a very new item. It was about four feet tall as opposed to the desktop scanners available today. Once the pictures were scanned in, they were processed by new graphics software on the computer and then the graphics were printed on the Xerox laser printer. This was a revolutionary event. They actually saw a computer printer print a graphic image. No one had ever seen anything but text printed on these printers.

At this same meeting, they saw the work that was being done in Ottawa to print parts catalogs for large telephone switches using this technology. They were very impressed. This looked like a very similar application to their catalog, although their document was much more complex and more frequently updated.

Upon their return from Canada, the team attempted to sell the user department on the potential of the new system using the new technologies that they had seen. Despite their efforts, there was no interest. Rather than dropping the idea, the IT department decided to propose the system themselves to the Steering Committee.

Questions for Discussion:

1. Should the Steering Committee move forward on this project without the support of the user?

2. What are the pitfalls for IT should the project be approved?

3. What do you think actually happened?

If you're curious about what really happened, please send me an email. My contact information can be found under the "Contact Me" section of my Web site, www.paulingevaldson.com.

Supplemental Reading

The ideas contained in this book were learned during my 40+ year career in IT and developed from a series of articles that I wrote between 2002 and 2010. The articles are listed below and links to each of them are available on my Web site, www.paulingevaldson.com, under the articles section.

It's Not Your IT Portfolio—It's Theirs, *CIO* magazine, December 9, 2002.

Alignment Is a Team Effort, *Computerworld*, May 24, 2004.

IT Survival Guide, *Computerworld*, August 23, 2004.

Chain of Command: IT and the CEO, *Computerworld*, May 23, 2005.

CEOs: Think Through Your CIO Choice, *Computerworld*, August 22, 2005.

IT Cheat Sheet for CEOs, *Computerworld*, September 26, 2005.

Seven People of Highly Ineffective Habits, *Computerworld*, January 23, 2006.

In Leadership, Little Things Count, *Computerworld*, May 22, 2006.

The Care and Feeding of Consultants, *Computerworld*, May 29, 2006.

The True Cost of Off-the-Shelf, *Computerworld*, July 31, 2006.

Security: It's the CIO's Job, *Computerworld*, August 28, 2006.

Getting In Sync, *CIO* magazine, September 5, 2006.

IT, We Have a Problem! *Computerworld*, November 27, 2006.

IT, We have a Problem! Part II, *Computerworld*, January 29, 2007.

What to Say to the CEO, *Computerworld*, April 23, 2007.

IT, We Have a Problem—Revisited, *Computerworld*, June 4, 2007.

Deciding Which Way to Decide, *Computerworld*, July 30, 2007.

No More Mr. Nice Guy: It's Time for IT to Say No, *Computerworld*, October 29, 2007.

Strategic IT Systems? There Are None, *Computerworld*, January 21, 2008.

Are You Delegating Enough? *Computerworld*, March 24, 2008.

Answering the Question, "Why Can't I Get Promoted?" *Computerworld*, September 29, 2008.

Top 10 Qualities of a Great IT Shop, *Computerworld*, December, 22, 2008.

Don't Blame Your Users for Their Ignorance about IT— Train Them, *Computerworld*, April 20, 2009.

Dazzle Your CEO with Hard Facts on ROI, *Computerworld*, June 22, 2009.

When IT Works with Users, It Benefits Everyone, *Computerworld*, August 10, 2009.

IT is Not the Mailroom, *Computerworld*, November 2, 2009.

Why Users Need to be Involved with IT, *Computerworld*, February, 22, 2010.

The U.S. Must Preserve Tech Competence, *Computerworld*, March 22, 2010.

Stopping the Technology Brain Drain, *Computerworld*, September 13, 2010.

About the Author

 **Paul Ingevaldson** discovered IT in 1965 working for Data Processing Consultants in Chicago. He retired at the end of 2004, completing forty years in the IT industry. During those years, he worked as a programmer, analyst, and systems manager at Sears; spent two years in the U.S. Army, ultimately repairing computers in Vietnam; and spent twenty-five years at Ace Hardware, becoming their first CIO and ultimately achieving the position of Senior Vice President of International and Technology for Ace. He has a Bachelor's Degree in Business (BBA) and an MBA from Loyola University in Chicago.

Since retirement, Paul has remained active in the industry, writing over thirty articles for *Computerworld* and *CIO* magazine, keynoting several IT conferences, guest lecturing in various Master's Degree classes at Northern Illinois University, conducting on-site seminars, and participating in several podcasts along with blogging for The Center for CIO Leadership and *The Digital Manufacturing Report*.

In his spare time, Paul engages in lifetime learning, primarily in the areas of science and world history. He is an avid amateur photographer and does a bit of traveling. As of this writing, he has visited seventy-five countries around the world.

CPSIA information can be obtained
at www.ICGtesting.com
Printed in the USA
BVHW032226060919
557675BV00002B/180/P

9 780615 651552